Contents

KT-591-131

How to use this study guide

Welcome to the New Testament – a strange and captivating world, removed from ours by over 2,000 miles and nearly 2,000 years. This New Testament study guide will help you find your bearings. It is no detailed roadmap, but it will show you the lay of the land and signpost the main destinations.

For each of the 27 books that make up the New Testament, you'll find a brief introductory section on the author ('Who?'), their core message ('What?') and how we can make sense of that message today ('So what?'). Before going through a particular book, you'll want to look at the corresponding introductory notes.

The section 'Questions to guide you' will keep you from losing the thread. Consider these questions while reading or listening to The New Testament.

Once you've completed a book, the sections 'For group reflection' will help you further explore its content with others. Alternatively, you can go through the questions on your own, though we recommend that you consider them as part of a group if possible.

Before you start, please take the time to read the Introduction on page 5. It will give you a quick but essential overview of the range of New Testament writings, and it will help you understand more of the historical and theological background against which they came into existence.

We wish you every blessing as you enter and travel through the world of the New Testament.

THE NEW TESTAMENT

An Introductory Study Guide

Michael Pfundner

Bible Society
Stonehill Green
Westlea
Swindon SN5 7DG
biblesociety.org.uk
bibleresources.org.uk

First published 2014 by The British and Foreign Bible Society.

ISBN: 978-0-564-04367-5

Production and typesetting by Bible Society Resources Ltd,
a wholly-owned subsidiary of The British and Foreign Bible Society

Cover design by Origin Design
Text design by Colin Hall, TypeFunction

Printed in Great Britain

Introduction

The story of Jesus

As far as we know, Jesus didn't leave any writings to posterity. It was left to others to write about him.

Four literary accounts, known as the **Gospels** of **Matthew**, **Mark**, **Luke** and **John**, have been handed down to us through the centuries. Between them, they make up roughly the first half of the part of the Bible we call the New Testament.

The Gospel stories are set in first-century **Galilee and Judea**, a backwater of the Roman Empire. Two and a half centuries before the Romans, Alexander the Great had had his stab at world domination. He exported Hellenistic culture to the far corners of his realm, including the Middle East. As a result, Greek was still the official language across the region even long after Alexander's empire had fallen apart. So it doesn't come as a surprise that the Gospels were written in Greek.

Scholars generally **date the writing** of Mark's Gospel to around AD 70, John around AD 90 and Luke and Matthew somewhere in between. In other words, the Gospels were probably written a generation or two after the events they report.

The story of Jesus, however, began to spread much earlier. At the end of his public ministry he had taken on the religious establishment in Jerusalem, which was one of the factors that led to his arrest and execution by the Roman authorities. Remarkably, within weeks of his death, his followers were once again declaring him to be the **Messiah**.

Messiah – 'Christos' in Greek, from which we get the word '**Christ**' – means 'the anointed one'. The Jews had waited for many years for a king like David to come and rule God's people once more. This messianic expectation was widespread at the time of Jesus, and anyone who named Jesus as 'Jesus Christ' was claiming that the crucified carpenter from Nazareth was the long-expected Messiah. But Jesus wasn't just called Messiah, he was also recognised as 'Lord'; by claiming 'Lordship' for Jesus the early Christians were in direct conflict with the Roman Empire, which maintained that there was no Lord but Caesar.

Then as now, Palestine was rife with political, ethnic and religious tension. Jews who resented the Roman occupiers built their dream of liberation on the advent of the **Messiah**; and it was not uncommon for a charismatic leader to gather supporters who put their messianic hopes in him. Neither was it uncommon for such a leader to challenge Rome and be killed in the process. Provided they escaped punishment, his followers may have decided to join another rebellion. One thing they were unlikely to do was to go round telling everyone that their former, executed leader had been the Messiah. But this is exactly what happened in Jesus' case. What conclusions can we draw?

Firstly, Jesus must have been a **historical figure**. Had he been a mythical invention, as some people would have us believe, Christians would have ensured that Jesus matched first-century expectations of what the Messiah would be like: a spiritual superhero with God on his side. To tell your fellow Jews that the Messiah was a former Rabbi, a craftsman from Galilee, who had managed to get himself killed like a common criminal by pagan idol-worshippers, would have been a fairly bad marketing ploy. Yet, that is precisely what Christians did. Why would they, unless they believed it to be true? Jesus of Nazareth, the Messiah, is simply too counter-intuitive to be an invention.

Secondly, to deny the Christian claim that Jesus **rose from the dead** makes it difficult to explain the birth of the Church. As he hung on a Roman cross, his disciples naturally concluded that his mission had failed. All they could do was to go into hiding and wait for things to blow over. Instead, they soon began to preach publicly in his name – the very people who had given up on him only weeks before. What, other than the resurrection of Jesus, could have brought about such a change of heart?

The message of Messiah Jesus soon attracted new believers. In a matter of decades, Christian fellowships could be found scattered across the Roman Empire.

To deliver their message, believers largely relied on the **spoken word**. They told the story of Jesus in personal encounters, synagogues and market squares, and recited his words wherever they gathered for worship or instructed new converts. But while Christian fellowships were springing up all over the place, the generation of Palestinian Jews who had met Jesus in person was beginning to die out; preserving the good news for those who would follow became a necessity.

The Gospel authors drew from the oral Church tradition. By the time they put pen to papyrus, a few decades had elapsed since the events they describe. But ask any D-Day veteran, and you'll find that they remember minute details of what happened 70 years ago. The early Christians were anxious to **preserve the authentic Jesus** as experienced by his first followers. In other words, no Gospel or other text made it into the New Testament unless it was regarded as the work of an apostle – one of Jesus' closest followers – or at least based on their testimony.

We don't know for sure who wrote the Gospels. Early Church tradition attributed them to **Matthew** and **John**, two of Jesus' 12 disciples; **Mark**, an associate of apostles Peter and Paul; and **Luke**, another friend of Paul's. Compare the four Gospels with **other texts about Jesus** – and there were plenty around at the time – and you can see why the latter failed to make it into the New Testament. Take the Infancy Gospel of Thomas, for example: it portrays the young Jesus as a mischievous lad equipped with magical powers who delights in using them at the expense of his adversaries. In the Gospel of Peter the risen Jesus is followed by a talking cross as he emerges from the tomb. And in the Gospel of Thomas the teachings of Jewish 'Rabbi Yeshua' morph to the mystical musings of a Gentile philosopher.

These so-called **apocryphal gospels** tended to be written much later than the four 'canonical' ones. And there is no question which of the two groups comes closer to reflecting the ministry and teachings of Jesus.

The story spreads

The four Gospels are followed by the Book of **Acts**, which starts off with the early days of the Church in Jerusalem and ends with the gospel message reaching Rome.

Christianity began as a **Jewish** movement. Jesus was Jewish. So were his first followers, who became the pillars of the early Church – foremost among them were Simon Peter, former fisherman turned apostle, and James, a brother of Jesus, who had come to believe in him. Neither Peter nor James simply severed their ties with Judaism when they became Christians.

Soon, however, a certain **Paul** of Tarsus began to preach Christ a long way off from Jerusalem and Palestine. Paul, whose missionary travels make up a large portion of the Book of Acts, became known as the apostle to the **Gentiles** (non-Jews).

Paul had not been one of the Twelve. But he knew Peter and James, the pillars of the Jerusalem church. Once he had founded the first congregations in Asia Minor (modern-day Turkey) and Greece, Paul was concerned that the new believers would stand firm in their faith. As he couldn't keep visiting them, he wrote to them instead. A number of **Paul's letters** survived and were preserved as part of the New Testament. You can find them after the Book of Acts. Paul outlines the hallmarks of Christian belief and how the faithful are to express that belief in everyday life.

Paul's epistles are followed by a number of **other New Testament letters**, which also deal with the basics of Christian faith and practice. Some of them take a somewhat different angle to Paul, thereby complementing the great apostle's writings. Even within the letters bearing Paul's name a careful reader will at times find different emphases. Taken together, then, the New Testament epistles show the breadth of early Christian teaching, as well as the priority items on the Church agenda.

Compiling the texts we now refer to as the New Testament was by no means a straightforward process. They were all written against the backdrop of **internal struggle** and **external threat**. Christians were still making sense of their beliefs, which meant they sometimes disagreed; and they were beginning to experience persecution.

Internal struggle arose once the young Church began to receive new converts from a range of religious and cultural backgrounds. Soon it found itself wedged between the Jewish and Greco-Roman cultures. People wrestled with their religious heritage: should they remain a Jewish movement or welcome Gentiles into the fellowship? Should they continue to observe the Old Testament laws, handed down by Moses? How could they reconcile their expectations of the messianic kingdom with the story of Jesus? None of these questions was straightforward.

The new faith met with opposition before long, and some of those **external threats** are tangible throughout the New Testament texts. They were not composed by reclusive scribes who had time to research, discuss and contemplate the life of Christ from the tranquillity of their study. To declare Jesus as Lord could be risky business at a time when loyalty to the State involved emperor worship. The thing to grasp is that Christians read Jesus' resurrection as the prologue to an apocalyptic drama: God was going to restore his oppressed people, establish his reign on earth and secure those who put their trust in Christ a place in his Kingdom. By raising him from the dead, God had vindicated Messiah Jesus and was going to put him in charge of everything and everyone, including Caesar. In other words, there was no way you could profess Christ as Lord and worship the Emperor at the same time. No wonder Christians were facing opposition and persecution before long.

Read, or listen to, the New Testament and you will begin to sense these internal and external tensions. Early Christianity was **diverse**, vibrant and on a religious and political tightrope; a living organism, threatened but thriving; a mixed group of believers, united by the same, explosive message: the good news of Christ.

The story culminates

The New Testament concludes with a glimpse of eternity: the **Book of Revelation**. It belongs to the genre of 'apocalyptic' literature, which crops up in the Old Testament on a few occasions, e.g. in the Book of Daniel. In New Testament times, apocalyptic texts were more widespread. The Dead Sea Scrolls of Qumran, discovered over half a century ago, bear witness to this fact: many of the scrolls contain **apocalyptic texts** that teem with exotic images. Their symbolism may be puzzling to us but would have made sense to readers at the time, certainly those on the inside. The same is true of the Book of Revelation.

Revelation was written during a period when professing Jesus Christ carried with it the distinct possibility of martyrdom. The author encourages believers to hold on to their faith, even in the midst of persecution, knowing that in the end God will wrap up human history and establish his **everlasting kingdom**.

The story that began in a small town, in an insignificant Roman province, draws to a triumphant close: God, ruler of the universe, who inaugurated his kingdom in Jesus, will reveal himself fully to a world that is out of kilter, and put it right for all time.

The Gospel of Matthew

Who?

The original Gospel manuscripts were not entitled 'Matthew', 'Mark', 'Luke' and 'John'. Their authors were not interested in making a name for themselves; they wanted to proclaim Jesus.

Early Church tradition believed that **Matthew**, one of Jesus' 12 disciples, had written the first of the four Gospels. His was thought to be the oldest of the four, which is why it is at the beginning of the New Testament.

For a number of reasons, however, most contemporary scholars think that **Mark predates Matthew**. Large sections of Matthew are strikingly similar to Mark, which suggests that one drew from the other. Matthew is more stylish and elaborate, so the 'simpler' Mark is more likely to have been Matthew's source, rather than the other way round. Matthew also contains material that cannot be found in Mark, so he may have had access to one or perhaps even several additional sources.

If it is true that Mark is older, the question is why would Matthew, who was one of the disciples, base his Gospel on Mark, who was not – unless of course Mark had used Peter's eyewitness testimony?

In the end, does it matter who wrote Matthew? Let's remind ourselves that, by the time the four Gospels were written, their authors were able to draw from a rich, carefully preserved body of stories about Jesus, his sayings and collections of fulfilled Old Testament prophecies showing him to be the Messiah. That Jesus **tradition**, in turn, was based on the witness of the apostles. So, in a sense, it is secondary whether the Gospel was written by the disciple Matthew or a second-generation Christian who had access to apostolic witness. It certainly wasn't important to the author; nowhere in the Gospel does he reveal his identity. He doesn't seek to promote himself but his Lord.

What?

Matthew's Gospel is steeped in the **Old Testament**: having been born in Bethlehem, the city of David, Jesus is the rightful heir of Israel's greatest king. In Jesus the messianic prophecies have been fulfilled. He has not come to do away with the Law of Moses, but to fulfil it and take it to a new level. Matthew even seems to have arranged the bulk of his material in five sections, which could be read as echoing the five books of Moses, the bedrock of Judaism.*

But Matthew is **not exclusively Jewish**. He is the only evangelist to include the magi from the East – pagan astrologers – in his account of the birth of Jesus. He ends his Gospel with the Great Commission: the risen Jesus commands his disciples to take his message to the far corners of the earth.

Matthew contains one of the most famous Bible passages: the **Sermon on the Mount**, which Luke only renders in part, while Mark and John leave it out altogether. The whole of Matthew puts great emphasis on practical Christian living.

So what?

Matthew appears to have written primarily for first-century Jews who believed in Messiah Jesus – a world from which we are far removed. Yet, Matthew's Gospel is **timeless** and speaks into our present-day reality.

Matthew is **for everyone**: his Gospel begins with non-Jewish astrologers worshipping the infant Jesus and ends with the risen Christ sending his disciples to the ends of the earth.

Matthew is the only Gospel to mention the word '**church**': the worldwide fellowship of believers that will prevail against the odds (Matthew 16.18).

Matthew reminds us that faith without obedience to **Christ's teachings** is worthless. The Christian life should be as counter-cultural as the Sermon on the Mount.

Questions to guide you ...

- Can you detect the major themes in the **Sermon on the Mount**?
- What do '**the Scriptures**' (the Old Testament) say about the Messiah?
- How do Jesus' **parables** describe the 'Kingdom of God'?
- What does Matthew say about the **end of time** and God's Kingdom?
- How does Matthew draw out the deeper meaning of the **death** of Christ?

 For group reflection:

- Who, according to Matthew, is **Jesus**?
- What, according to Matthew, is a **church**?
- What, according to Matthew, is the **Kingdom of God**?

The Gospel of Mark

Who?

The early Church believed that the author of this Gospel was Paul's associate, John Mark, and that he had heard the story of Jesus when **Peter** was preaching in **Rome**. As is the case with Matthew, modern scholars tend to remove Mark further from Jesus' innermost circle. They do, however, generally regard his Gospel as the oldest of the four and therefore closest to the events.

Mark evidently wrote for **non-Jews**. He explains details of Jewish faith and culture which are noticeably absent from Matthew's 'Jewish' Gospel. He also uses some Latin terms, which suggests that his audience may have been Roman.

What?

Mark starts off by stating his subject, 'the good news of **Jesus Christ, the Son of God**': he will be writing about a real person (Jesus), who is the Messiah (Christ) and more than a man (Son of God).

Mark's fast-paced narrative echoes the urgency of **the Messiah's mission**: to herald the coming Kingdom of God; to call people to repent and live according to Kingdom standards; to heal the sick and work miracles, symbolising victory over evil and pain; to cleanse the temple, foreshadowing the final renewal of God's people; to suffer and give his life; to overcome death.

Mark doesn't offer neat solutions but holds things in **tension**: Jesus is both man and 'Son of God'; he is the Messiah but he has to suffer; he predicts the coming Kingdom of God but gives no definite timeline of end-time events; he rises from the dead, but the resurrection account is mysterious and sketchy.

So what?

Mark serves as a helpful reminder that, in Jesus, we are dealing with a **God who is not like us** breaking into our world; we should not be surprised that this Jesus is radically different to our thoughts, feelings and expectations. When dealing with the Son of God, trying to be either too clever or too chummy will lead to disappointment.

Mark's Gospel is not just about the radical 'otherness' of God. Mark makes the point that Jesus was also **truly human** – not some divine phantom – and can empathise with the human condition. As the author of the Letter to the Hebrews puts it, 'now that Jesus has suffered and was tempted, he can help anyone else who is tempted' (Hebrews 2.18).

While Mark cannot be squeezed into our categories of Western, rationalist thinking, he invites us to embrace the gospel message as powerful and real, nonetheless. Mark emphasises the **call to discipleship**: to follow Jesus is radical, costly and infinitely rewarding (see Mark 10.29–30)

 Questions to guide you...

- Can you spot some examples of Mark explaining the first-century **Jewish world** to his readers? How does this help your understanding?

- Where and how does Mark stress the **humanity** of Jesus?

- Where and how does he indicate the **divinity** of Jesus?

- How is the message of **God's Kingdom** to affect the way we behave? Listen out for hints in chapters 1, 9, 10 (on two occasions) and 12.

- What parallels can you spot between Mark's account of Jesus' crucifixion and the following **Old Testament** passages?

  'when I was thirsty, they gave me vinegar.'

  (Psalm 69.21)

  'They took my clothes and gambled for them.'

  (Psalm 22.18)

  'Others thought he was a sinner, but he suffered for our sins and asked God to forgive us.'

  (Isaiah 53.12)

  'On that day, I, the LORD God, will make the sun go down at midday, and I will turn daylight into darkness.'

  (Amos 8.9)

For group reflection:

- How does **Mark's** overall portrayal of Jesus compare to **Matthew's**?
- Reflect on Jesus' call to **discipleship** (e.g. Mark 10).
- Mark's original **resurrection account** is thought to have ended at verse 8. Those eight verses may not give us much detail; but do they still contain all we need to know? Discuss.

The Gospel of Luke

Who?

The third Gospel may have been written by '**our dear doctor Luke**' (Colossians 4.14), a friend of Paul's who accompanied the apostle for part of his missionary journeys. As with Matthew, however, Luke seems to have drawn extensively from Mark; and his take on Old Testament Judaism seems more conciliatory than Paul's – both of which might suggest a different author to the 'dear doctor'. At any rate, the evangelist emphasises how he consulted with eyewitnesses to ensure that his Gospel would be a reliable foundation for his readers on which to build their faith.

Luke addresses his Gospel to **Theophilus**. Was this an individual recipient? Or was it a synonym for Christian believers ('Theophilus' meaning 'God's beloved') who would read Luke's report?

What?

Both Mark and Paul highlight the **contrast** between the order of Old Testament Judaism and the radically new message of Jesus, whereas Luke, like Matthew, tends to emphasise the **continuity** between the two. Note that these authors don't contradict but complement one another.

From the outset Luke places the gospel message in the context of secular **history** – the Roman Empire – and **God's story** with his people, initiated in Old Testament times and now fulfilled in Jesus.

Luke stresses the **inclusive** nature of the gospel: it is for Jews, Gentiles and people on the margins of Jewish society and religion, such as women, the poor or the neighbouring Samaritans.

As with the other Gospels, Luke contains some exclusive stories, found nowhere else in the New Testament. We owe some of Jesus' most famous **parables** – the Prodigal Son and the Good Samaritan – to Luke's careful study of everything that took place (Luke 1.3).

So what?

Jesus' messianic inauguration speech (Luke 4.16–30) summarises the thrust of Luke's Gospel: a **message of hope** for those who have none.

Luke inspires us to think about the **social implications** of the gospel, which is not only about eternity and individual salvation, but also about applying God's Kingdom standards in the here and now.

Luke gives us a helpful guideline for daily **Christian living**: a life of hope, reconciliation and love for the marginalised.

 Questions to guide you ...

- Where does Luke detect common ground between **Jews and Christians**?
- How, according to Luke, can you be both a good Christian and a good **Roman** citizen?
- What does Jesus say on **wealth and poverty**?
- What do we learn about the **Holy Spirit** in the life of the believer?
- Mark's **passion** narrative is rather terse; Luke tends to pay more attention to detail. Listen out for information Luke provides on Jesus' suffering and death that cannot be found in Mark.
- Luke's **resurrection** account shows Jesus displaying both human and non-human features. Can you detect them?
- Luke focuses less on the sacrifice of Jesus and more on his **victory over death.** Can you detect the difference in emphasis?

 For group reflection:

- How can we apply Luke's sense of inclusiveness to living as Christians in a **pluralistic society** today?
- What can we glean from Luke's emphasis on **hope and justice**?
- What strikes you about Jesus' **prayer** life?

The Gospel of John

Who?

As is the case with the other three Gospels, the **author** does not state his name.

Second-century bishop, Irenaeus, linked the fourth Gospel with **John, the disciple**. Bishop Papias referred to **John the Elder**, who had been based at the church in the city of Ephesus. They may or may not have been talking about the same person.

John's Gospel is rooted in first-century **Judaism**. There are references to the Old Testament and the Messiah; the author knows his way round Jerusalem and Palestine; and although written in Greek, the Gospel displays traits of Aramaic. In other words, apart from the Hellenistic (Greek style) Prologue (John 1.1–14), John is never far from the world of the Old Testament.

What?

Scholars group Matthew, Mark and Luke together as the '**synoptic Gospels**'; their perspectives of Jesus are strikingly similar. John's Gospel is another matter.

The Synoptics share a lot of material between them. Some of it is found in the fourth Gospel, but large sections are **exclusive to John**.

John contains a number of long **discourses** and debates with the Jewish leaders that don't appear in the Synoptics.

Many of the synoptic accounts are set in Galilee. John focuses on Jesus in **Jerusalem**.

Above all, John puts greater emphasis on the **divinity** of Jesus than the Synoptics.

So what?

John gives us a **universal and eternal** perspective of the gospel: it transcends all boundaries of religion, culture, ethnicity and time.

John speaks into the situation of **the Church**, then and now, picking up key themes like unity among believers, the role of the Holy Spirit or persecution by the enemies of the gospel.

More so than the Synoptics, John can open our eyes to the **divine** nature of Christ.

The Church gave John the symbol of an **eagle**, as if to say that, theologically, John soars above the Synoptics.

 Questions to guide you ...

- What images does John use to describe Christ in the **Prologue** (John 1.1–14)?

- What passages in John can you remember from **Matthew**, **Mark and Luke**? Why might John have selected them among the wealth of Jesus stories recorded in the Synoptics?

- Jesus performs **seven** 'signs'. Can you spot them?

- John records a number of '**I am**' sayings of Jesus – a turn of phrase reserved for the God of the Old Testament. Can you identify those sayings? Which one do you find the most helpful?

- Can you find other instances in John that underline the **divinity** of Jesus?

- We said earlier that John contains references to the **Old Testament**. Can you spot any?

- The term '**love**' appears 27 times in the Synoptics but 38 times in John alone. Can you detect a pattern in the way John defines love?

 For group reflection:

- Which portrayal of Jesus do you find more accessible: **John's** or that of the **Synoptics**?

- How can John and the Synoptics, taken together, give us a **more complete picture** of Jesus?

- John tends to refer to Jesus' **miracles** as signs. What might they signify?

Acts

Who?

Both the addressee and the writing style in **Luke's Gospel** and **Acts** (also known as The Acts of the Apostles) are identical, so we can safely assume that the two books were written by the same author.

Luke dedicates his second report to **Theophilus**, tracing Church history from its beginnings to the point where it begins to spread across the eastern Mediterranean.

What?

Acts continues in the same vein as Luke's Gospel ended: the Jesus message is for **Jews and Gentiles** alike.

Acts describes the birth of **the Church** at Pentecost, its clash with Judaism and its decision to preach Christ beyond the geographical and religious boundaries of Jerusalem and the Holy Land.

Acts tells us about the **conversion of Saul**, a zealous Jew and persecutor of Christians. Following his vision of Jesus, Saul asks to be baptised and goes on to become the greatest Christian missionary in antiquity.

The second half of Acts is devoted to the **missionary journeys** of the apostle Paul that take him across Asia Minor and Greece and end with his arrival in Rome. Midway through Paul's travels we find the author of Acts at his side; the narrative voice changes from 'they' to 'we'.

So what?

Acts shows how, from the outset, the Church was confronted with internal and external **conflict**. There never was such a thing as an ideal, original Christianity. We are encouraged to proclaim the gospel nonetheless.

Acts emphasises the role of the **Holy Spirit** in the life of the Christian; as witnesses to the gospel, we are not on our own.

In an individualistic age like ours, Acts reminds us that Christians are to live in close **fellowship**, devoted to each other and looking out for one another.

Questions to guide you ...

- What are the hallmarks of God's plan of **salvation** according to Peter's sermon at Pentecost (Acts 2)?
- What were the hallmarks of **Christian fellowship** in Acts 2?
- How does the story of Cornelius (Acts 10) symbolise the rift between Jews and **Gentiles**, and the way God heals it?
- How does Paul's engagement with people differ, depending on whether they are **Jews or Gentiles**?
- How does the **Holy Spirit** 'engage with' the preaching of the good news?

 For group reflection:

- What can we **learn from the early Christians** about courage, stamina and missionary zeal?
- What can we learn from the first Christians about taking the gospel into a **multicultural** environment?
- Acts emphasises **God's guiding hand** in the history of the Church. How might this translate into the life of the Church today?

Romans

Who?

The letter to the Romans is **'classic Paul'**; it is here that he treats his core theological themes in greater depth than elsewhere.

The **recipients** were the Christians living in Rome during the mid first century, less than a decade before the Emperor Nero began to persecute them.

The Christians in Rome appear to have been a mix of believers of **Jewish and Gentile** origin.

What?

In Romans, Paul is greatly concerned with **divine justice**: God's holiness, his dealing with evil, his offer of salvation for both Jews and Gentiles, and his guidelines for a Church that is called to reflect his flawless character.

Secondly, Romans deals with **human righteousness**: it cannot be earned by obeying the Law of Moses – seeing as everyone falls short of it – but must be received as a gift through faith in Jesus Christ.

Paul sets out to show how the gospel bridges the gap between **Jews and non-Jews**. In Jesus, God extends his grace to the Gentiles, even though, previously, they weren't part of God's covenant and never had access to the Mosaic Law. This, however, does not mean that God has abandoned the people of Israel. Even though they are rejecting Jesus, they are still at the heart of his salvation plan: 'In this way all Israel will be saved' (Romans 11.26).

So what?

The letter to the Romans can help us get a better grasp of how God deals with the **problem of evil** – the evil around us and the evil within us.

Romans can help us appreciate and embrace the heart of the good news; faith in Jesus is the key to having **peace with God**.

In Romans national, ethnic and religious **differences** are viewed under the all-encompassing grace of God, offered to those who put their faith in Christ. The church in Rome was diverse; conflict was inevitable. The gospel of universal grace showed, and still shows, a way out.

 Questions to guide you …

- What are Paul's key points on **God's righteousness**?
- What are Paul's key points on **human sin**?
- What are Paul's key points on **justification by faith**?
- Paul shows that Christ is the end point of the Mosaic Law (Romans 10.4). Does this mean we can do as we please, so long as we say we have faith? To help you explore this, make a bullet point list of Paul's **instructions for Christian living** (Romans 12 to 14).
- How do we make sense of Paul's teachings on **the State** (Romans 13) in today's world?
- The final chapter gives a long **list of names**. See whether that list might give you any clues on the make-up of the Christian church in Rome, e.g. the role of women in mission and ministry.

 For group reflection:

- If we are **saved by faith**, and Old Testament laws (e.g. purity laws, sacrifices or festivals) are no longer valid for Christians, how are we to interpret Paul's comment that, rather than doing away with the Law, faith upholds it (Romans 3.31)?
- How do we make sense of the promise of **freedom from sin** for Christians living by the power of the Holy Spirit, while believers still find themselves struggling with sin (Romans 7 and 8)?
- How are we to understand Paul's command in Romans 12.1–2 to be '**a living sacrifice**'? What could this mean in practice, in your life, your church?

1 Corinthians

Who?

Despite generating some interest in his message in the Greek capital, Athens (see Acts 17), Paul apparently failed to found a church there. Not so in **Corinth**, where people came to faith as a result of his ministry.

Paul appears to have penned **several letters** to the Corinthian church, two of which survived and were included in the New Testament canon – the list of books accepted by the Church as inspired and authoritative.

Corinth was a thriving city, and its upwardly mobile inhabitants appear to have viewed life rather differently to an average, law-abiding Hebrew. Their religious and ethical views were apt to put off any self-respecting Jew for good.

What?

1 Corinthians addresses **doctrinal issues**, such as the Lord's Supper, the Holy Spirit and the resurrection of the dead.

1 Corinthians addresses **moral issues**, such as disputes among Christians, ethical standards and the practice of Christian love.

1 Corinthians addresses **cultural issues**, such as Greek philosophy, religion and sexual ethics.

So what?

With its emphasis on human wisdom, achievement and liberty, ancient Corinth posed challenges similar to the ones Christians face in **today's Western culture**. This makes 1 Corinthians one of Paul's most immediately accessible writings.

1 Corinthians gives us valuable insight into **church practice** and Christian living.

1 Corinthians gives us **hope**, helping us to focus on the transforming power of the Holy Spirit, of Christian love and of the resurrection day when believers will finally be united with Christ.

Questions to guide you ...

- How does Paul view **human philosophy** in regard to divine revelation?
- How does the Corinthian view of the **body** compare to Paul's Judeo-Christian stance?
- What does Paul say about the role of the **Holy Spirit** in the life of the Church?
- What evidence does Paul give for the **resurrection** of Jesus?
- Which Corinthian **issues** do you think are especially pertinent to today's Church?

 For group reflection:

- If Paul were to write to **your church**, what cultural, spiritual or moral issues might he address?
- How might you apply **1 Corinthians 13** to the life of your church?
- At the time he wrote this letter, Paul appears to have expected the return of Christ in the lifetime of at least some of his readers (1 Corinthians 15.51). How are we meant to live faithfully in the '**already but not yet**' – the time between the past inauguration of God's Kingdom through the resurrection of Jesus and its final implementation on the day Christ returns to earth?

2 Corinthians

Who?

As with 1 Corinthians, Pauline **authorship** is well attested by the early Church. Paul's own reference to another letter suggests that 2 Corinthians followed a previous, now lost, epistle written between 1 and 2 Corinthians. Moreover, 1 Corinthians 5 mentions a letter preceding 1 Corinthians. In other words, Paul appears to have written four letters, of which the first and third have been lost.

Paul's **audience** is the same as in 1 Corinthians, except that things have gone from bad to worse.

What?

2 Corinthians suggests that Paul is **losing control** over a church which is in danger of departing from the original gospel message.

Paul devotes much of this letter to defending his **apostolic authority** against critical voices and competing, influential teachers in the church at Corinth.

He stresses the contrast between his calling as an apostle and his own **weakness** and sufferings for the sake of Christ.

The middle section of 2 Corinthians deals with a **practical matter**: Palestine had been struck by a famine in AD 49, and Paul is asking the Christians in wealthy Corinth for support.

So what?

2 Corinthians is honest about the **cost of discipleship** and of being a leader. It sets us thinking about the reality of suffering in the life of the faithful.

The letter offers **comfort** too. In the midst of affliction, weakness and seeming defeat, God's power is at work in us.

Half a century after Paul, Bishop Clement of Rome pointed out that the Corinthian church was still grappling with the same issues as in Paul's day. 1 and 2 Corinthians remind us to be realistic about the '**human factor**', as well as trusting that God will achieve his purposes through and sometimes in spite of us.

Questions to guide you ...

- Paul often starts a letter by thanking God for the **faith of his readers**. How does this compare to his opening prayer of 2 Corinthians?

- In Jewish thinking the **temple** was synonymous with the presence of God. How does Paul reinterpret this idea in the light of the gospel (2 Corinthians 6)?

- How might Paul's instructions on **giving** (chapters 8 and 9) be applied to our day?

- 'My power is strongest when you are weak' (2 Corinthians 12.9) is one of Paul's frequently quoted phrases. What do you think it means?

 For group reflection:

- What are the main lessons to be learnt from Paul's **hardships**?

- How might the struggles at Corinth help your church to avoid **similar issues**?

- How can we **stand firm** in our faith, no matter what challenges are thrown at us?

Galatians

Who?

Like Romans, Galatians is a treatise on **law and grace**, on faith and works, against the backdrop of translating a Jewish message for non-Jews.

The letter is addressed to no particular church, but most likely to believers across southern Galatia, now south-eastern **Turkey** – a region through which Paul travelled on the first of his three missionary journeys.

What?

As in 2 Corinthians, Paul's apostolic authority is at stake. **Christians from a Jewish background** sought to undermine his position; they objected to his claim that believers in Jesus were no longer obliged to observe the Law of Moses.

Paul is alarmed by the fact that Christians in Galatia have introduced Old Testament Law into their new faith and practice. He reminds them that Christians have entered into a **new covenant** with God, which is solely based on the divine grace offered to them in Jesus Christ. You don't need to be a Jew to be a Christian.

God's grace does not imply that Christians can live as they please, so long as they profess to believe. They are under a new master: not the Law, but the **Holy Spirit**, who will transform their character and behaviour, producing 'spiritual fruits' of love and holiness.

So what?

Galatians, alongside Romans, was the blueprint for the **Reformation**. Not by good works – which in sixteenth-century Europe essentially meant Church law – but by faith in God's grace do we enter into a relationship with him.

Paul says: 'Faith in Christ Jesus is what makes each of you equal with each other, whether you are a Jew or a Greek, a slave or a free person, a man or a woman' (Galatians 3.28). Paul seems to be talking about **spiritual unity** – every Christian being part of God's family – not about social equality or human rights; and yet, it is intriguing to think how revolutionary Paul's statement must have sounded to his audience and how pertinent it still is for a Church, and indeed a world, divided over issues of gender, social class, religion or race.

Few passages in Paul's writings sum up the **Christian life** as succinctly as: 'God's Spirit makes us loving, happy, peaceful, patient, kind, good, faithful, gentle, and self-controlled. There is no law against behaving in any of these ways' (Galatians 5.22–23).

 Questions to guide you …

- What were **Paul's opponents** teaching? There are several things that crop up at different points in the letter; make a note of them.

- Why is Paul so **harsh** towards people who may just see things a little differently?

- Try to sum up the points Paul makes about **Abraham** (Galatians 3) and later on **Sarah and Hagar** (Galatians 4).

- In the final two chapters (Galatians 5 and 6), how does Paul seek to ensure that the Galatians don't **misinterpret the gospel of grace** as a carte blanche to live as they please?

 For group reflection:

- Since Paul spends much of the final part of his letter on instructions for **righteous living**, what does it mean to be saved by faith and grace alone?

- Discuss **Galatians 3.28** in the context of both your church and the wider culture. What practical steps might your fellowship take in applying more of the equality in Christ that Paul is talking about?

- Galatians is a fairly **angry** letter. How does this square with Paul's list of the 'fruits of the Spirit' (Galatians 5.22–23)?

Ephesians

Who?

Ephesus was known both for its academic status and its veneration of Artemis, the Greek goddess of fertility. The ancient city was situated on the west coast of what is now Turkey, and its remains can still be admired today. The apostle **Paul** ended up in prison after challenging the Ephesian Artemis cult.

Scholars are divided over the **authorship** of this letter. It may be based on an earlier, no longer extant, Pauline epistle, and therefore still bear Paul's name despite the final version having been penned by someone else. The same is true of the letter to the Colossians, which partly overlaps with Ephesians in content. Even if Paul were not the author of the final version of these letters, God would have been free to inspire whichever other writer he chose. That said there are experts who believe Paul to be the author of both Ephesians and Colossians.

What?

Ephesians contains some powerful **images**.

It uses the image of a **dividing wall** (between Jews and Gentiles) having been broken down when they came to believe in Christ.

It speaks about the Church as the **body of Christ**.

The relationship between Christ and his Church is likened to that between **husband and wife**.

A further metaphor for the Church and her Lord is the relationship between **master and slave**.

In the final chapter, we encounter a **military image**: the Christian is likened to a Roman soldier in full armour, ready for battle.

So what?

In recent years, Ephesians 6 has been widely used as a blueprint for '**spiritual warfare**'. This can be both helpful and misleading. As with any other metaphor, the imagery taken from Roman combat requires cautious interpretation.

Questions to guide you ...

- How does the prayer at the end of chapter 1 characterise **the risen Christ**?
- How does Ephesians 2 sum up the relationship between **Jewish and Gentile** Christians?
- What are the hallmarks of a church built on **Christian principles** (see chapter 4)?
- Try to paraphrase the analogy between the Church and **marriage**.
- Try to paraphrase the analogy between the Christian life and **warfare**.

 For group reflection:

- Reflect as a group on the theme of **unity** in the Church, expressed through the image of the body (see Ephesians 4).
- Discuss ways of engaging with the wider **culture** without pandering to it (see Ephesians 5).
- Explore the theme of **spiritual warfare** (Ephesians 6) in the light of what else the letter says about a Christ-centred life.

Philippians

Who?

Paul is writing to the Christian church in Philippi, in northern **Greece**. The fellowship started out as a house church which Paul had founded (see Acts 16).

What?

Philippians 2.6–11 introduces the idea of kenosis, of **God emptying himself.** In Jesus, God became man, which means he put aside divine attributes like omnipotence or omnipresence. Paul may be quoting a hymn that was already in existence by the time he wrote the letter.

Philippians stresses the **joy** of being a Christian, regardless of our circumstances. Note that, as he says in the letter, Paul is in prison at the time of writing!

Paul reminds the Philippians that, despite the comfort and joy of faith, we are not meant to rest on our laurels but are called to ongoing **spiritual growth**.

So what?

Philippians 2.6–11 can help us to appreciate more deeply the meaning of the **incarnation** – God showing his love by becoming human in Jesus.

Paul introduces the passage above by exhorting his fellow-believers to have the same attitude as Christ, **letting go** of power and status for the sake of love and service.

Philippians is an antidote for '**cheap grace**' (a term coined by German theologian and Nazi opponent, Dietrich Bonhoeffer). Paul stresses the fact that simply to say 'I believe in Jesus' is not enough. We are to 'work with fear and trembling to discover what it really means to be saved' (Philippians 2.12). The great apostle himself goes on to say: 'I have not yet reached my goal, and I am not perfect. But Christ has taken hold of me. So I keep on running and struggling to take hold of the prize' (Philippians 3.12).

Questions to guide you ...

- Listen out for the contexts in which Paul refers to **joy**; why should we be joyful?
- How does Paul's **introductory prayer** compare to, say, 2 Corinthians or Galatians?
- What are Paul's **priorities** in life?
- How does Paul depict the **incarnation** (God becoming human) in chapter 2?
- In chapter 3 Paul summarises in a few verses what he describes at length in Romans and Galatians: to **live by grace**, rather than under the Law. Can you list the main points?

For group reflection:

- Reflect on Philippians 2.1–11; how are **identity and self-denial** connected?
- Discuss Philippians 2.12: 'work out your own salvation with fear and trembling' (NRSV) and 3.12: 'I have not yet reached my goal, and I am not perfect. But Christ has taken hold of me. So I keep on running and struggling to take hold of the prize' (CEV). How do these verses square with Paul's teaching on **salvation by grace**? Try looking at them in the context of the respective passages in which they appear.
- Consider Paul's words on **peace** (Philippians 4.7) in the context of the Jewish concept of 'Shalom' and the Christian expectation of Christ's return.

Colossians

Who?

The church at Colossae had been founded by a fellow-missionary of Paul's, named **Epaphras**. The city, which no longer exists, was located in Asia Minor (modern-day Turkey), to the east of Ephesus. As with Ephesians, some scholars believe that at least parts of Colossians may have been penned by a later follower of Paul, rather than the apostle himself.

What?

The letter attacks the '**Colossian heresy**'; the believers seem to have focused heavily on feasts and angel worship.

Colossians urges believers to be **heavenly-minded** and live pure lives dedicated to God.

The letter does not challenge slave ownership; the goal is not **social change**, but for people to lead Christ-like lives, whatever culture they live in.

So what?

Colossians may challenge us to ponder the question: how might **worldviews** running counter to the gospel undermine our faith today?

Tackling the Gnostic belief in 'creator-angels', Colossians elevates the '**cosmic Christ**' through whom God has made the world, and

> 'in whom are hidden all the treasures of wisdom and knowledge.'
>
> (Colossians 2.2–3, ESV)

The letter helps us to think of Christ in broader terms than personal salvation.

Colossians can serve as a reminder that Christians should be heavenly-minded, leading **radically different** lives as a result.

Questions to guide you ...

- Make a list of the traits of the '**cosmic Christ**' in chapter 1.

- Try to identify the **Jewish and Gnostic** teachings that Colossians 2 warns against.

- What are **the key characteristics** of the Christian life (see Colossians 3)?

- What does Colossians say about '**household rules**'?

- Which **names** in the closing section of Colossians do you recognise from other parts of the New Testament?

For group reflection:

- Try to apply the '**Colossian heresy**' to our modern-day context.

- Consider the 'household rules' at the end of chapter 3 and the instructions for slaves and masters in Colossians 4.1; discuss the difference between **timeless** biblical truths and **culturally restricted** teachings.

- Prayerfully reflect on the '**cosmic Christ**' (Colossians 1).

1 Thessalonians

Who?

The apostle Paul may well have written this letter soon after visiting the **Macedonian city** of Thessalonica, from where he was driven out during a riot, along with his missionary colleague, Silas (see Acts 17). 1 Thessalonians may be the first of Paul's letters, which would make it the earliest book of the New Testament – the text closest to the time of Jesus that we possess.

What?

1 Thessalonians provides the basis for what some nowadays refer to as the **'rapture'**. In Greco-Roman tradition, people went out to meet their king as he entered the city after a victorious battle. Paul picks up this image and applies it to the **Second Coming** of Christ.

Remarkably, Paul doesn't elaborate on his key theme, justification by faith. Instead, he focuses on Christ's Second Coming and admonishes the believers to lead godly lives in anticipation of the Lord's return.

A large part of the letter is devoted to Paul's **close relationship** with the Thessalonian church. What a contrast to some other letters, like 2 Corinthians or Galatians!

So what?

1 Thessalonians is a source of **comfort** in times of bereavement and grief. Paul reminds his readers that death cannot separate fellow-believers forever.

The letter puts great emphasis on the **end of time**: a vision of hope and a call to responsible living.

As ever, the apostle's own example sets a high standard for both **missionary zeal** and **pastoral care**.

Questions to guide you ...

- Paul is delighted that the Christians in Thessalonica are **growing in their faith**. Make a note of the signs of spiritual growth (see chapter 1).

- Once again, Paul seems to have had his **critics**; how does he defend his apostleship?

- Summarise Paul's main points on the **return of Christ**.

- What, according to 1 Thessalonians, are the hallmarks of **Christian conduct**?

 For group reflection:

- What are the main points Paul makes concerning **Christ's return** in glory?

- At the time of writing 1 Thessalonians, Paul appears to have expected Christ to come back to earth in his lifetime. Did he get his **timing** wrong? If he did, would it matter?

- Discuss Paul's attack on the **Jews** (1 Thessalonians 2.15–16) in the light of what he says in other places, e.g. Romans 11. What do you make of one scholarly view that these verses may have been inserted by a later author?

2 Thessalonians

Who?

2 Thessalonians finds the church in a **different situation** to 1 Thessalonians. The tone is less positive. Expectation of Christ's imminent return has led some believers to live idle lives. And the church has been suffering persecution.

What?

The letter addresses individuals in the Thessalonian church who claim that the Parousia – the **Second Coming** of Christ – has already taken place (perhaps in some mystical form), as well as those who appear to have given up work and their ordinary lives in expectance of Christ's imminent return.

2 Thessalonians gives us a '**timetable**' of Christ's return in glory. This will be a visible, as opposed to mystical, event preceded by a final showdown between God and the forces of evil.

There is a reference to the '**wicked one**' or 'man of lawlessness'. Early Christians thought him to be Nero, whereas the sixteenth-century Reformers believed the passage to be a prophetic reference to the Pope.

So what?

2 Thessalonians can help us to strike a **balance** between eagerly expecting God's Kingdom and becoming so heavenly-minded that we end up being of no earthly use.

Paul is under no illusion that **suffering and evil** are integral parts of our earthly existence. But it doesn't end there. Paul picks up the teaching of Jesus: God is still in charge and his Kingdom is coming.

Questions to guide you ...

- Watch out for the hallmarks of the **Second Coming** that have previously cropped up in other parts of the New Testament: God's Kingdom, judgement, salvation, etc.
- How does the **suffering** of the Thessalonians fit into the context of God's judgement and the future glory?
- Try to sum up the struggle of **good versus evil** at the end of time.

 For group reflection:

- **Compare** 1 Thessalonians 4.13—5.11 with 2 Thessalonians 2.1–12. Each passage responds to a different question and therefore has a different emphasis. Try to identify the two angles from which Paul is coming.
- Now, with the passages above in mind, revisit **1 Corinthians 15**. Compare the key points in all three passages.
- How do the descriptions of the Parousia in the passages above compare with popular **end-time predictions** that endeavour to fix the date of Christ's return?

1 Timothy

Who?

This is the first of three letters known as the '**Pastoral Epistles**': 1 and 2 Timothy and Titus. They are addressed to individuals, not churches. Both Timothy and Titus were co-workers of Paul's. Timothy was based at the church in Ephesus, while Titus was serving in Crete.

The Pastoral Epistles were written at a time when churches had become more **established and organised**, so much so that some scholars regard the 'Pastoral Epistles', or at least parts of them, as the work of a later follower of Paul's. We have to leave the debate to the experts, confident that, irrespective of human authorship, these writings rightfully belong in the canon of Scripture.

What?

Once again, Paul feels obliged to address **false teachings**. Once again, we have evidence that early Christianity was developing and diverse.

Chapter 2 includes a famous passage that combines Jewish monotheism ('one God') with the Old Testament concept of **ransom**:

> 'Christ Jesus, who gave himself as a ransom for us all'.
> (1 Timothy 2.5–6, ESV)

The letter stands out on account of its detailed instructions for **bishops** (also translated as 'overseers') and **deacons**.

1 Timothy is (in)famous for its enigmatic reference to **women** being saved by childbirth and its seemingly negative attitude towards women – though some scholars would argue that it is not as negative as is sometimes believed.

The letter closes with Paul's **personal advice** to Timothy.

So what?

The first letter to Timothy contains some brief key passages that help us to grasp the **essence of the Christian faith**: Christ, mediator between God and humanity (2.5); Christ, the ransom for our wrongdoings (2.6); Christ, who reveals God 'in the flesh' (3.16, ESV).

The letter is full of practical instructions for **Christian leadership** and **church relationships**. It offers guidelines to each generation on how to run a church according to New Testament principles.

Though it may not make comfortable reading, the letter needs to be included in any discussion on the role of **women in Christian ministry**.

 Questions to guide you ...

- What kinds of **issues** did Timothy have to grapple with in the Ephesian church?

- List Paul's key points on **prayer**.

- What are the hallmarks of a godly **leader**?

- What does Paul have to say about **material wealth**?

- Take note of examples where Paul is dealing with **false doctrine**, and which topics he is addressing in particular.

 For group reflection:

- According to some – though certainly not all – scholars, 1 Timothy appears to tackle the influence of an early form of **Gnosticism** on the Ephesian church (e.g. reference to '[Gnostic] knowledge' in 1 Timothy 6.20). Gnosticism reinterpreted Genesis 3 ('The Fall') as Adam not having been seduced but enlightened by Eve when she handed him the fruit from the Tree of Knowledge. As a group, consider **1 Timothy 2.9–15** as a possible response to the Gnostic take on women. Does this change what on the surface reads like a blueprint for male supremacy? Might Paul's command that a woman should not teach be restricted to the women in the Ephesian church who, influenced by Gnosticism, may have been teaching female supremacy?* Share your views as a group, bearing in mind that the influence of early Gnosticism on the church is disputed among scholars.

- Consider 1 Timothy 2.15: 'But women will be saved by having children if they stay faithful, loving, holy,

* Points 1 and 2 for group discussion – source: Bruce Barron, 'Putting women in their place: 1 Timothy 2 and evangelical views of women in church leadership.' *Journal of the Evangelical Theological Society* 33.4 (1990) 451-459. In www. ntgateway.com

and modest.' The Greek word for 'being saved' can also mean being '**healed**' or '**protected**'. Having just spoken of Eve's sin and subsequent curse resulting, among other things, in painful childbirth, might Paul be reassuring married and pregnant women in the fellowship of God's protection? *Discuss!

- As a group, **meditate** on this verse:

  'He was revealed in flesh, vindicated in spirit, seen by angels, proclaimed among Gentiles, believed in throughout the world, taken up in glory'.

  (1 Timothy 3.16, NRSV)

2 Timothy

Who?

2 Timothy would have been **Paul's last letter,** written
to a fellow-minister of the gospel and friend. Timothy
had formerly joined the apostle on his second missionary
journey (see Acts 16) and was now in charge of the Christian
congregation in Ephesus. The second letter is even more
personal than the first. Two of Timothy's nearest and
dearest are mentioned by name. Paul speaks of his isolation
in prison and approaching death. He urges Timothy to visit
him soon and – an emotive detail – not to forget to bring
Paul's coat and scrolls.

What?

Attacked by his opponents and abandoned by some of his
former friends, Paul is **in prison**, expecting execution. Yet,
he is more concerned about Timothy than himself.

Paul speaks of **finishing the race** of faith, passing on the
torch to his fellow-missionary and waiting to receive the
wreath of glory.

Paul urges Timothy to follow his example in fighting the
good fight as 'a good **soldier** of Christ' (2 Timothy 2.3).

So what?

2 Timothy reminds us to view our life from the point of
finishing well, and what might need to happen now to
ensure we don't look back one day and realise that we didn't
'run the race' as we should have done.

The letter helps us to grasp the **cost of discipleship** – both
as we read Paul's instructions to Timothy and as we consider
Paul's sufferings for the sake of the gospel.

As ever, we are encouraged not to cling to the here and
now, but to live in **anticipation** of what is yet to come.

Questions to guide you ...

- Take note of the context in which Paul speaks of (not) being **ashamed**.
- Listen out for the parallels Paul draws between faith and **military service**.
- What are the attributes of a **good workman**?
- What are the hallmarks of the '**last days**'?
- How could **Paul's instructions** to Timothy be summed up?

 For group reflection:

- What does the letter say about **perseverance** in faith?
- What does it say about being **faithful to the truth** of the gospel?
- Look at **2 Timothy 3.16**, preferably not just in the CEV, but another translation that sticks closer to the original wording (such as the NRSV, for example). Can this verse be used to proof-text biblical inspiration, biblical inerrancy and the like?

Titus

Who?

Tradition regards Paul as the author of this letter. The addressee, Titus, a convert of Gentile origin, had been appointed **Bishop of Crete.**

What?

Titus himself is to appoint **church leaders**. Paul lists their necessary qualifications, making practical Christian living a main theme of this letter. Once again, slaves are told to submit; the early Church was concerned with proclaiming the gospel, not social change.

So what?

Titus provides valuable insight into what a **Christian church** should look like: followers of Christ are to live according to their Lord's teachings, thereby drawing the attention of outsiders to the transforming power of the gospel.

The letter also contains a reminder of **Christ's return** in glory and the need to live righteously in anticipation.

 Questions to guide you ...

- What are the qualifications expected of a **bishop**?
- What does the letter say about the conduct of **ordinary church members**?
- What are Paul's concerns regarding the faith of the Cretan believers being undermined by **false doctrine**?
- How does Paul describe **God's transforming work** in the believer?
- How are Christians to **treat their leaders** and itinerant preachers?

 For group reflection:

- Reflect on, and try to interpret, Paul's words on **spiritual rebirth** (Titus 3.4-7).

- Discuss Paul's instructions for **righteous living** in the light of his general emphasis on salvation by faith. Do the two complement each other, or is there a genuine tension?

- How is your church already aiming to be a **good witness** to outsiders? Where might there be room for improvement?

Philemon

Who?

Paul wrote this short letter to Philemon, a **fellow-Christian** and member of a house church. Paul was in prison at the time of writing, presumably in Rome.

What?

Slaves were common in Paul's day. Not all of them lived in misery. While still considered their master's property, slaves could rise to a position of responsibility and status.

Philemon's slave, **Onesimus**, had run off, apparently with some of his owner's money. Then he met Paul, who led him to faith. Paul is pleading with Philemon to forgive Onesimus, now that he has become a Christian and is willing to return to his master.

So what?

Once again, we are challenged to follow **Paul's example**: even as a prisoner, he is willing to forget about his own problems and focus on helping others.

Paul is normally not known to mince his words. Note his unusually **diplomatic** approach as he seeks to help a fellow-believer.

The letter exemplifies Paul's famous words on **Christian unity** across all barriers (Galatians 3.28). Paul reminds Philemon that his superior social status and rights as a slave-owner must be subject to the fact that Onesimus, the slave, has become a member of God's family and a brother in Christ.

 Questions to guide you ...

- What do we learn about Paul's relationship with **Philemon**?
- What do we learn about Paul's relationship with **Onesimus**?
- This letter comes close to Paul suggesting that **fellowship in Christ and slavery** don't go together. Try to follow Paul's careful line of argument.

For group reflection:

- Is Paul **asking too much** of Philemon? How would you have reacted?

- **Onesimus'** willingness to return to his master was not without risk; explore his possible inner journey.

- How does the letter exemplify the 'higher justice' of **grace**? How could this principle be applied to your life/ your church?

Hebrews

Who?

We don't know who wrote the letter, nor do we know that it was originally a letter. Neither can we identify the recipients with certainty. Hebrews has been previously attributed to various authors, including characters as diverse as Luke, Priscilla and Apollos (see Acts 18). Significantly, Paul, who was long considered to be the most likely candidate, has been ruled out by modern scholarship. Third-century Church Father, Origen, concluded that **only God knew** who had penned Hebrews. It seems he was right.

What?

Hebrews draws from the world of Jewish priesthood, presenting Jesus as the great **high priest** who is superior to any earthly priest and indeed to any human or angelic being.

The letter derives its line of argument from the Jewish sacrificial system. On the annual Day of Atonement, people sacrificed animals to have their trespasses forgiven. Hebrews shows Jesus to be the **perfect sacrifice**.

Hebrews refers to the 'cloud of witnesses' (Hebrews 12.1, ESV) in the Old Testament: the **heroes of the Jewish faith** who have gone before the Christians, setting an example of perseverance and unconditional loyalty to God.

So what?

Like Paul, the author of Hebrews views Jesus through an **Old Testament** lens. Hebrews' emphasis on priesthood, however, is not found in Paul, whose main focus is on justification and reconciliation. Hebrews complements our understanding of salvation in Christ.

The letter raises our awareness of Christ's **supremacy and majesty** and can keep us from reducing him to 'my best friend, Jesus', 'being in love with Jesus' and the like.

Hebrews is a challenging letter, emphasising **God's holiness and wrath**. Some verses appear to suggest that it is possible for a Christian to lose their salvation. However we interpret them, they lead us to a deeper appreciation of the need to persevere on the journey of faith.

Questions to guide you ...

- The ancient Church came to define Christ as both **God and man**. How is this mystery expounded in Hebrews?

- How does chapter 2 link the incarnation (God becoming human in Christ) with **priesthood** and **atonement**?

- What does the letter say about the value of **animal sacrifice**?

- Paul elevated God's promises and **new covenant** above the former covenant with Israel. Can you spot parallels in Hebrews?

- Despite the letter's overall emphasis on God's holiness, Hebrews 4.16 encourages Christians **to approach God's throne boldly**. Are there other instances where the writer picks up this theme?

- Hebrews describes faith as a **journey** and **pilgrimage**. Can you spot references to the Exodus, the Old Testament journey of the people of Israel?

- Christians lived, and still live, in the tension of **God's Kingdom** breaking in through Christ and not yet having come in its fullness. Listen out for instances where the author of Hebrews refers to this tension between 'already' and 'not yet'.

- How is the expectation of **God's judgement** to affect the way Christians behave?

 For group reflection:

- What do we make of the language of **sacrifice** in an age that rejects the idea of God being placated through the spilling of blood?

- Can Christians **lose their salvation**? Consider and discuss Hebrews 6.4–6 and 10.26–31. Note that the phrase 'decide to sin' (Hebrews 10.26) is peculiar to the CEV translation. The Greek original, however, suggests an ongoing rebellious attitude towards God, as opposed to a momentary bad decision.

- Hebrews 13.20–21 summarises the writer's message of grace: it cost Jesus his life and is therefore not to be regarded as **cheap grace**. Explore these verses as you recap the main themes of Hebrews and the Old Testament metaphors used to illustrate them.

James

Who?

While Jesus had two **disciples** of that name, traditionally the author has been seen as one of his **brothers** (see Mark 6.3), though this is by no means certain. As for the recipients, James is vague, addressing the 12 tribes in the diaspora. He metaphorically alludes to the 12 tribes of Israel that were scattered by their enemies.

What?

German reformer, Martin Luther (1483–1546), dismissed James as an 'epistle of straw'. In his view it muddied the waters of Paul's **gospel of grace**.

Depending on their interpretation, people will side or disagree with Luther, and assert that James either contradicts or complements Paul. The bone of contention is found in chapter 2: James insists that we are not saved from God's judgement by faith alone, but also by doing **good works**.

So what?

Like Hebrews, James is an antidote for superficial faith. As with love that deserves the name, **genuine faith** is not about lip service or fuzzy feelings but involves mind and will as it increasingly drives and shapes our entire being. In this respect James in no different to any other biblical author, including Paul. The gospel is fundamentally a message of God's free gift of grace. Yet, nowhere in the New Testament are we told to take lightly the teachings of Christ, the severity of sin or the holiness of God.

Questions to guide you ...

- James is a distinctly **Jewish** text. Can you list the Old Testament characters and their significance to James' argumentation?
- How does James view **faith in action**?
- Make a list of topics on which James offers **practical advice**.
- Can you spot parallels between James and the **teachings of Jesus**?
- Explore the **social dimension** in James; what is his take on the divide between rich and poor?

 For group discussion

- What, according to James, are the hallmarks of a **mature Christian**?
- Consider his words on **repentance** (James 5.16–20) in the light of your previous group discussion on Hebrews 6.4–6 and 10.26–31.
- Was Luther right to **dismiss James** as an 'epistle of straw'?

1 Peter

Who?

Traditionally, the letter is associated with the great **apostle**. Some have argued that it is unlikely that a Galilean, Aramaic-speaking fisherman could have written the polished Greek that is found in the letter, though it is worth noting that even in the letter itself Peter mentions that a man named Silvanus helped him write it. The Christian churches among which it was circulated were scattered across what is now central and eastern Turkey.

What?

1 Peter picks up an Old Testament passage (Isaiah 53) on the **suffering servant**, by whose wounds we are healed, and applies it to Jesus.

Peter urges believers to **stand firm** in their faith, reminding them of Christ's example.

Structurally, 1 Peter echoes the writings of **Paul** in combining the theology of the gospel of redemption with practical instructions for Christian living.

So what?

1 Peter is a moving document that reminds us of the **courage** the early Christians were called to show in the face of persecution. It inevitably raises the question: would we 'be glad for the chance to suffer as Christ suffered' (1 Peter 4.13)?

1 Peter stands between the threat of persecution and the hope of Christ's return. In the meantime, Peter encourages believers to get on **with practical Christian living**.

Questions to guide you ...

- Despite the disquieting backdrop against which it was written, 1 Peter begins on a **joyful** note. Why?

- How does Peter describe and define the **holiness** of God and his people in chapters 1 and 2?

- Peter approaches the subject of **suffering** from various angles. Can you identify them?

- **Church leaders** were the most likely to become martyrs for their faith. Try to read between the lines of Peter's instructions for leaders in chapter 5.

 For group reflection:

- Peter shows great **empathy** for fellow-believers who have come under pressure from unsympathetic authorities. How might we follow his example with regard to modern-day persecution of Christians around the world?

- The early Church had no choice but patiently to bear the yoke of persecution. How does this compare with living as Christians in a modern, **democratic state** that is under the rule of law? Has the modern context changed our Christian stance and responsibility?

- Explore the imagery of the **temple** in 1 Peter 2.1–10 and the status of believers in Christ.

2 Peter

Who?

The **authorship** of 2 Peter is disputed. None of the Church Fathers mention the letter, at least explicitly, until the third century. 2 Peter appears to deal with second-century Gnostic teachings. It differs from 1 Peter in style. It also seems to have incorporated parts of the letter of Jude, which an apostle of Peter's stature would have seen no need to do. On the other hand, Jude may have been inspired by Peter, rather than vice versa. And in some respects the context in which the letter was written fits the lifetime of Peter.

What?

Like a number of other New Testament writings 2 Peter warns against **false teachers**.

The letter stands out by speaking of believers **partaking of Christ's heavenly nature**.

The **delay of the Second Coming** is explained by 'divine mathematics': for God one day is as a thousand years and vice versa (2 Peter 3.8).

So what?

While addressing issues of its day, 2 Peter conveys **timeless principles** for the Church, such as the need to discern true from false doctrine or warnings against the urge to establish a date for Christ's return.

Questions to guide you ...

- How does the opening of the letter sum up the relationship between **faith and works**?
- 2 Peter gives a long description of what characterises the **false teachers**. Try and distil the main points.
- How should the expectance of **God's judgement day** affect the way we live?

 For group reflection:

- Consider **2 Peter 1.4**: 'so that [God's] nature would become part of us', or, as more literal translations put it, we would become participants in, or partakers of, the divine nature (cf. NRSV, NIV, ESV). As a group reflect on the meaning of this verse in its context (verses 3–11).

- 2 Peter responds to Christians who were getting impatient and beginning to doubt whether **Christ would return**. How do we make sense of the fact that almost 2,000 years later the Second Coming has still not happened? Consider 2 Peter 3.8 in this context.

- If you were to write a circular letter to churches in Britain today, what **competing ideas and worldviews** would you warn them against? Is there a way of positive engagement with other faiths and philosophies, rather than outright rejection?

The letters of John

Who?

According to Church Fathers Polycarp and Irenaeus, the writer of **John's Gospel** also penned these **three letters**, two of which are so brief and similar in theme that we shall be considering all three together. It is worth noting, however, that some scholars think that 2 and 3 John were not written by the same person as 1 John, though they may have emerged from the same community.

What?

Another Church Father, Jerome, reported how John had become so old and frail that he had to be carried to the meeting place, where he kept preaching the same message: **love one another**. Indeed, love is at the heart of these letters.

John's concept of love, however, is not to be mistaken for universalism. The dualism of **dark and light** which already occurs in John's Gospel re-emerges in the letters. Those who deny that, in Christ, God became human (as the Gnostics did, because they thought that God could not be tainted by matter) place themselves outside the fellowship of love.

2 John warns against the **Antichrist** – the one who denies the incarnation.

3 John, the shortest book in the New Testament, is a brief, **private letter**.

So what?

John has been called the apostle of **love**. The famous words, 'God is love', are by him (1 John 4.8). It is worth studying this core theme of John's epistles and its significance for both theology and church practice. We need to be aware at all times that, according to John, those who resist God's truth cut themselves off from his love.

Questions to guide you ...

- How does the opening of 1 John respond to the Gnostic view that, given the base nature of matter, Jesus could not have been **truly human**?
- How does John link love with the theme of **light versus darkness**?
- How does he connect love with **holiness** and **Christian fellowship**?
- How does he describe **divine love**?
- What does it mean **to love God**?
- What is the **dividing line** between light and darkness, life and death (see chapter 5)?
- How does **2 John** encapsulate 1 John?
- According to **3 John**, what are the main things that Gaius is meant to observe in order to live as a true Christian?

 For group reflection:

- **Compare** the opening of 1 John 1 with the Prologue to John's Gospel (John 1). What similarities can you detect?
- Discuss practical ways of expressing, and growing in, the **love** that John is talking about.
- Can you square John's emphasis on love with his outright **condemnation** of those who reject Christ's dual nature (divine/human)? Discuss!

Jude

Who?

The author introduces himself as the **brother of James**. As he does not specify which James, he may well be referring to the one everybody knew, or at least knew about: James, the leader of the Jerusalem church, who was a brother of Jesus. This would make Jude one of Jesus' brothers too.

Jude is writing to believers whose faith is being undermined by **false teachers**.

What?

Jude is warning his readers against **heresy**. False teachers are questioning the 'orthodox' view of Christ, possibly from a Gnostic viewpoint, as well as preaching a form of antinomianism: sin as much as you like, for God will forgive you anyhow (see verses 4 and 16).

Jude evokes drastic **Old Testament** examples to illustrate the seriousness of what is going on in the Church: Hebrews rebelling against the Lord even after having been delivered from Egypt, Balaam being tempted to curse Israel for financial gain, Korah rebelling against Moses and Aaron, Cain murdering his brother Abel and God's judgement on Sodom and Gomorrah.

Jude also uses **extra-biblical sources** to make his point. The reference to the archangel Michael, Moses and the devil may well be based on a source named 'The Assumption of Moses'. Jude also quotes from 1 Enoch. Neither of these texts are part of the biblical canon, but they were obviously familiar to Jude and his readers.

So what?

Bad teaching can lead to bad living. Jude reminds us how **orthodoxy** (the right teaching) and **orthopraxis** (the right way of living) must go hand in hand.

Questions to guide you ...

- Listen out for the ways in which the **false teachers** have gone astray.

- Make a list of the **things Jude tells believers to do** in order to stay on the straight and narrow.

- The letter teems with **Old Testament** references. Can you spot them?

 For group reflection:

- In order to back up his arguments Jude used sources outside what is now the Old Testament. Discuss how we might benefit from **extra-biblical writings** today.

- In what way is Jude's characterisation of the false teachers applicable to our largely secular culture? How might we constructively **engage with our culture** without having our faith undermined in the process?

- Discuss Jude's allusions to **hell** and your response to them.

Revelation

Who?

Writing from the eastern Mediterranean island of Patmos, the author introduces himself as **John**. The difference in style may indicate that he is not the author of John's Gospel or the three Johannine letters. There may be more than one author, but the theological perspective is the same. Revelation is replete with apocalyptic imagery, which suggests that, unlike us, John's audience was familiar with it.

What?

While the book's title suggests the disclosure of what is unknown, **modern readers** can find its ancient symbolism all but incomprehensible.

Preachers tend to focus on the more accessible **opening and concluding chapters** of Revelation: Jesus rebuking various Christian fellowships for their shortcomings in chapters 2 and 3, and John's vision of Judgement Day and the New Jerusalem in chapters 20–22. The chapters in between can seem an even greater exegetical minefield than the famous ending.

Revelation combines the **genres** of epistle (letters to seven churches) and apocalyptic prophecy.

So what?

Though addressed to specific congregations, Revelation 2–3 is a timeless guide to **what kind of church** will please, or displease, the Lord.

Revelation draws our attention from the physical world to the heavenly dimension. It reminds us that our earthly struggles can be closely related to the **spiritual battle** raging between God and the forces of evil.

Revelation paints a grand picture of **eternity**, encouraging believers to remain faithful to God and not to lose sight of what is still to come.

Questions to guide you ...

- What are the **setting and context** of John's writing of Revelation?

- In what way are six of the **seven churches** in Revelation 2–3 flawed?

- What makes the church at **Philadelphia** special? What are they to look out for? What are they promised?

- How does Revelation 6 deal with **evil and death**?

- What are the key elements of **judgement and salvation** (Revelation 7–9)?

- As John homes in on the battle against the forces of evil and the **great divide** between God's faithful and the followers of Satan, what are the key images he uses to depict this struggle? Note that the number 666 (Revelation 13.18) has been interpreted in different ways, e.g. as a secret code for the Emperor Nero or a symbol of imperfection that falls short of number 7, which represents the divine. The apocalyptic showdown of Armageddon (Revelation 16.16) evokes the ancient Jewish battlefield of Megiddo.

- Make a note of what the final chapters of Revelation say about the **end of the world** as we know it.

For group reflection:

- Time and again, Revelation has been misused by people who turned it into a precise **end-time schedule**. Are there better ways of drawing meaning from Revelation today?

- Over the centuries, Christian focus shifted from God's reign on earth to God in heaven – the place where the souls of believers would go when they died. Do the final chapters of Revelation justify such a shift? What does John have to say about the **new earth**?

- How, if at all, has Revelation changed your view of **eternity**? How might this affect the way you live in the here and now?

Where do you go from here?

Congratulations on completing your journey through the New Testament! We hope you found it an enriching, perhaps even transforming, experience.

This study guide was designed to help you get a better grip on the New Testament, approaching each book from three angles: the author and their audience, the content of the book and what the text might be saying to us today. These three interpretive angles – author, text and reader – are vital for biblical interpretation.

One way of continuing your biblical journey is Bible Society's group resource, lyfe – **lyfe.org.uk** – designed to help you seek a richer relationship with God through the Bible and in the company of others.

For any questions about Bible Society resources and programmes, visit the website – **biblesociety.org.uk**

There are also a range of modern and traditional Bible translations available.

We at Bible Society would really value your feedback, so please don't hesitate to get in touch. Please email us at **contactus@biblesociety.org.uk**

We look forward to hearing from you!